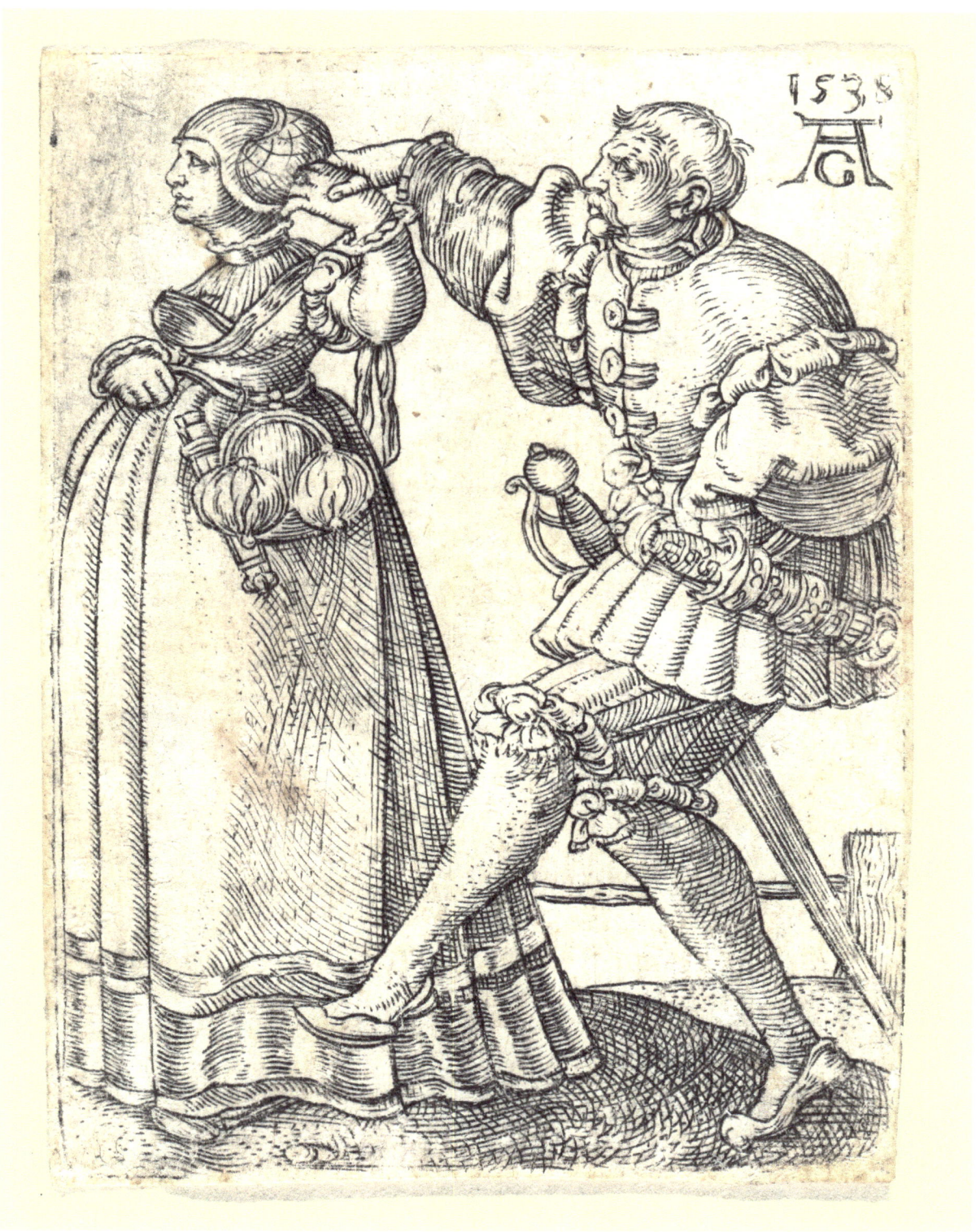

**This delightful book is made possible by the
generous public domain access from the New York Public Library.
The pictures are taken from etchings created and published by
Heinrich Aldegrever (German, 1502-ca. 1561) (Printmaker)
in the years 1538 and 1551.**

**This book was put together by
Don Landes-McCullough**

Parasol Publishing
1300 SE Park Crest Avenue
Vancouver, WA 98683

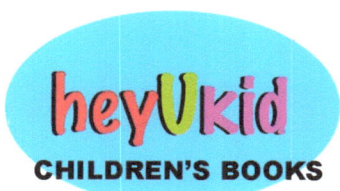

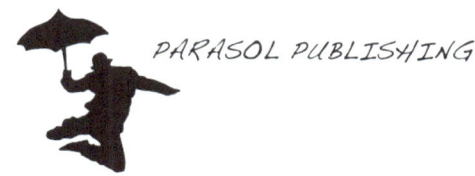

Available through Amazon.com, CreateSpace.com and other retail outlets.

3 1538

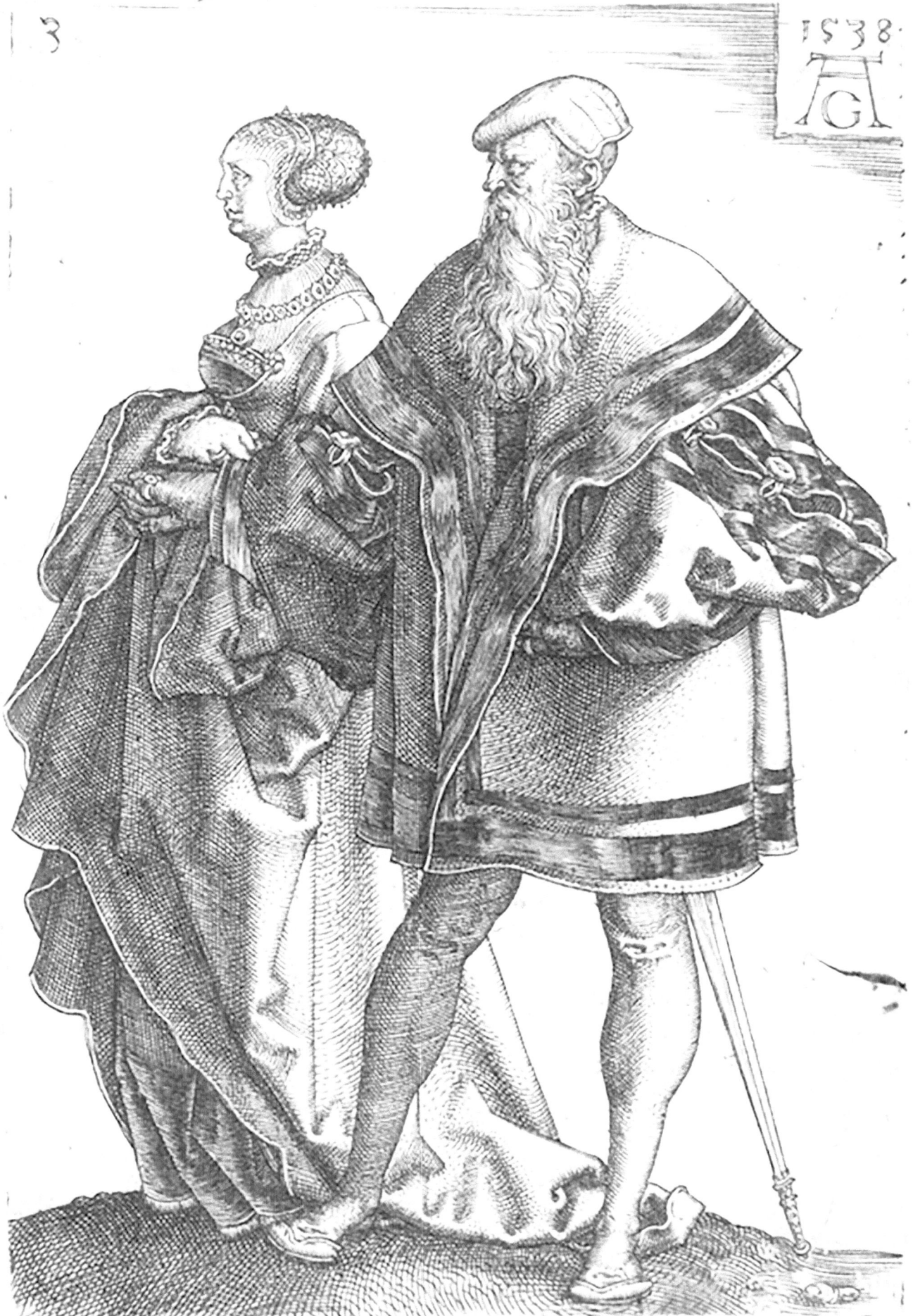

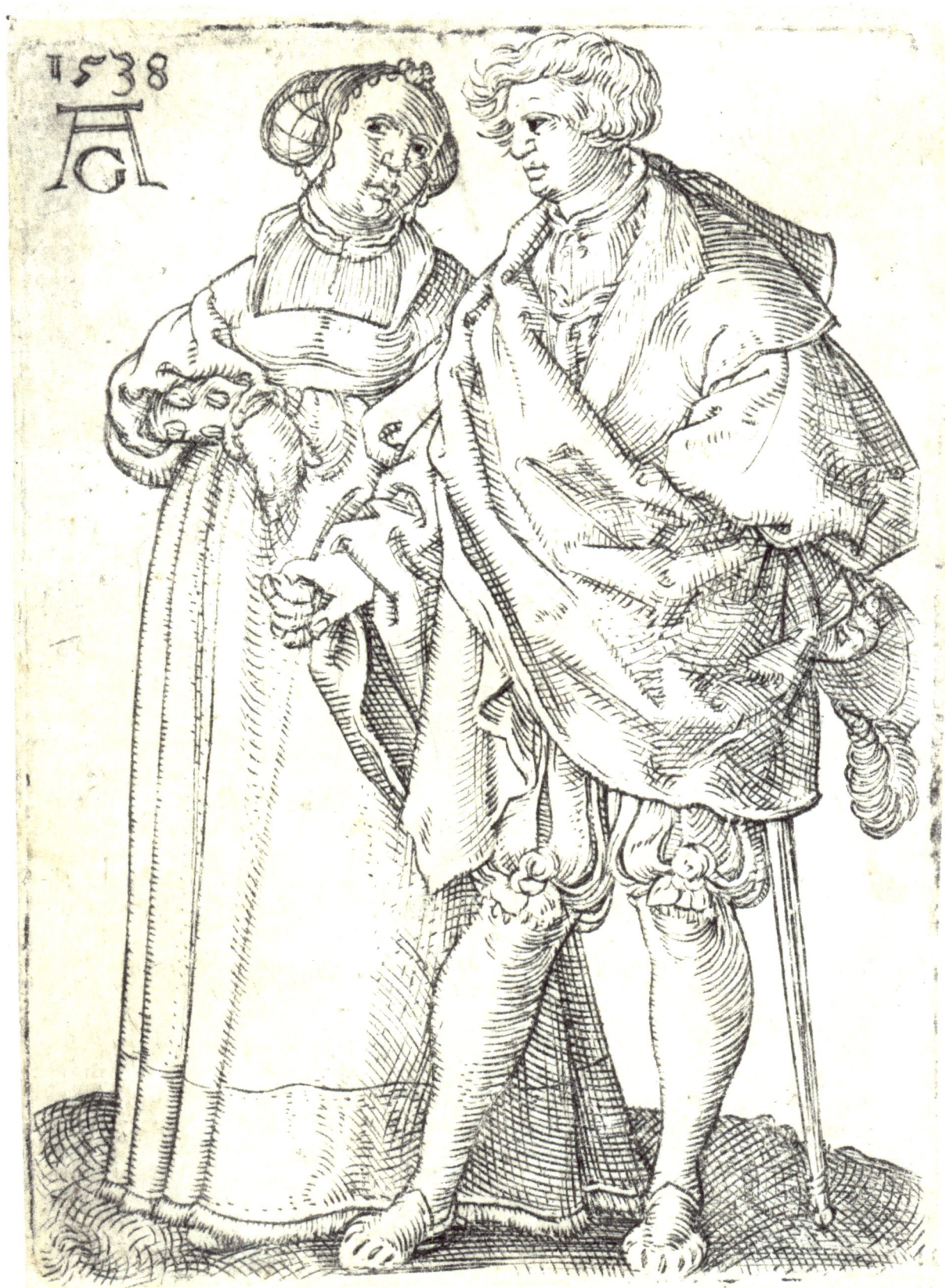

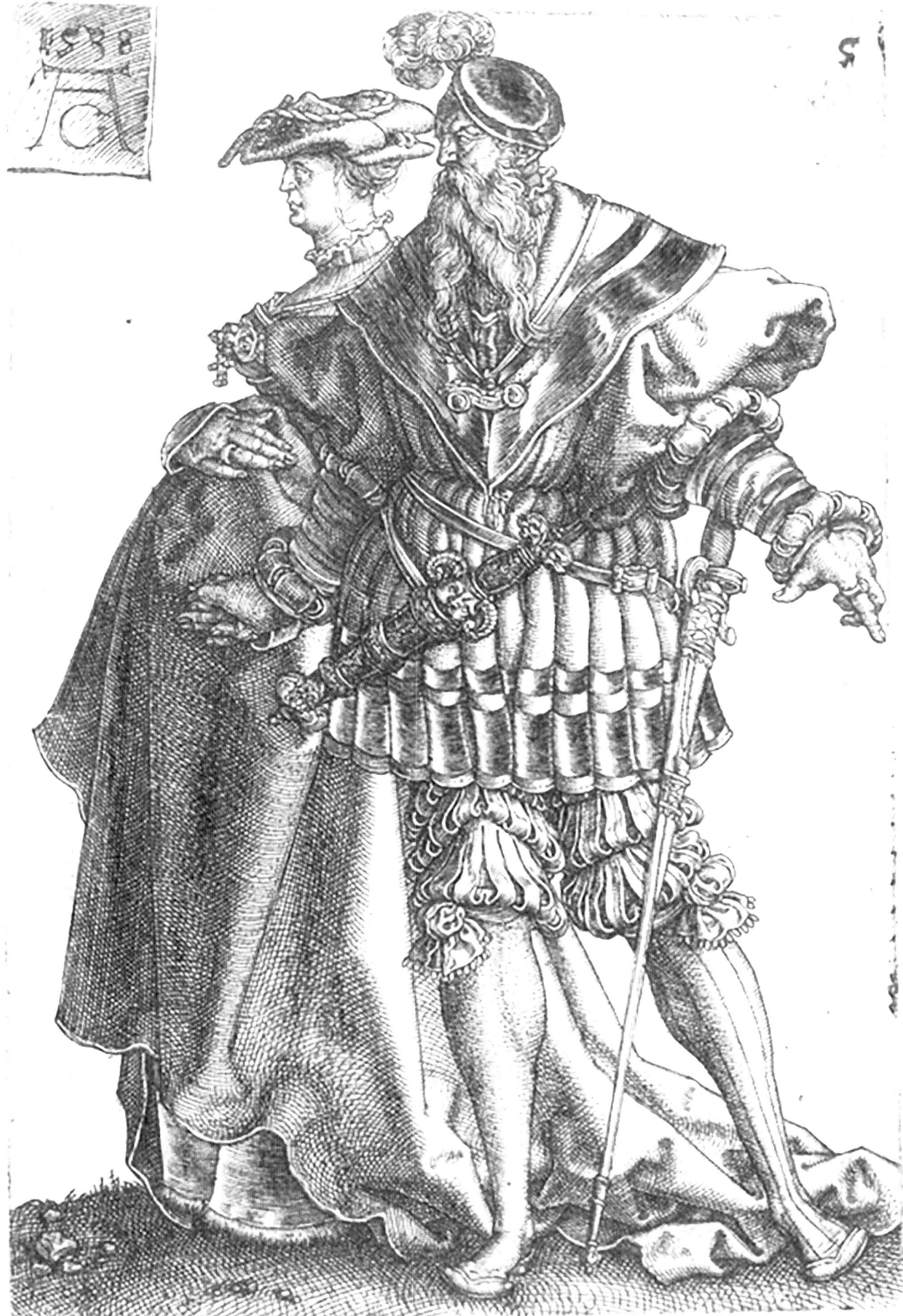

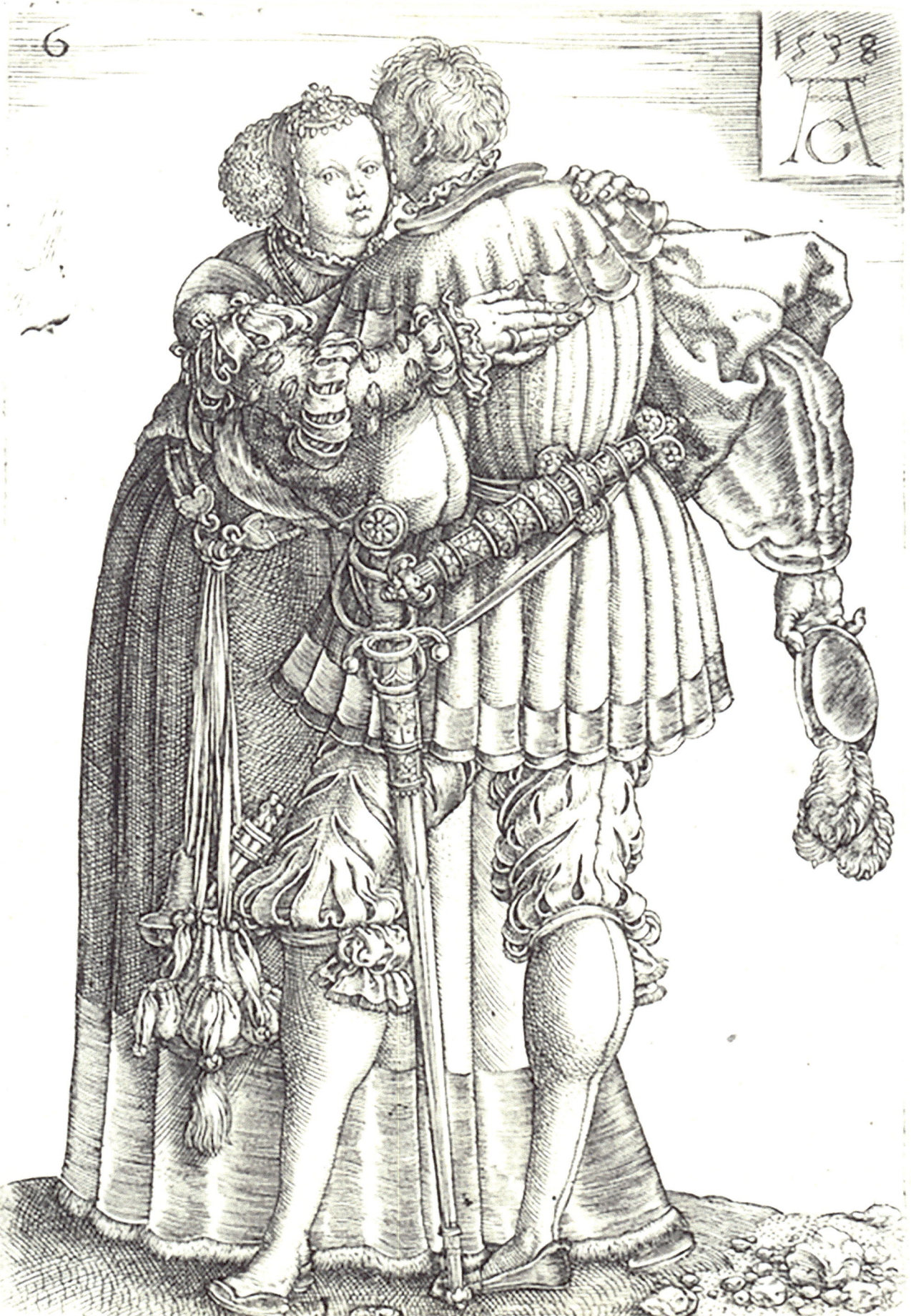

1538

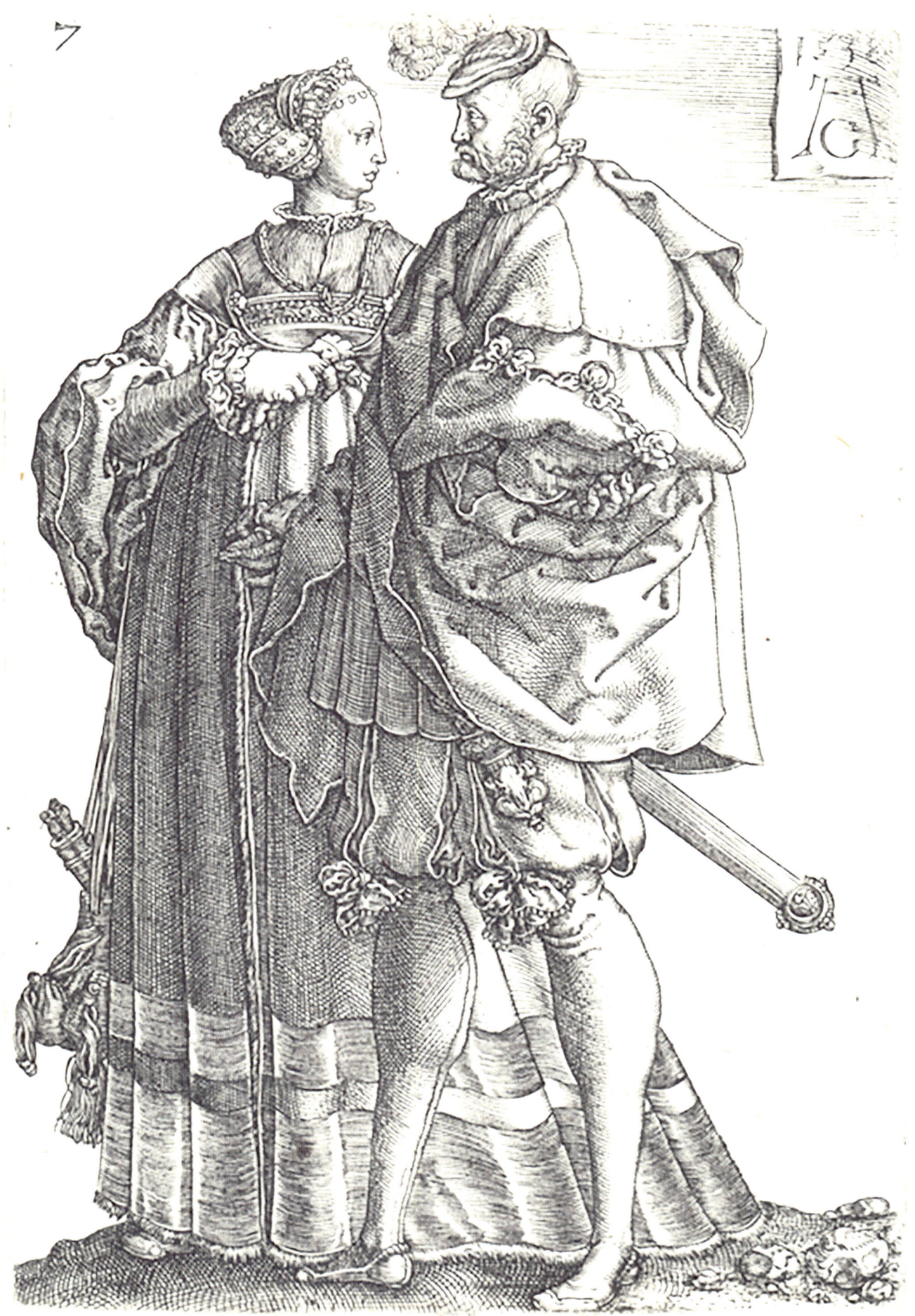

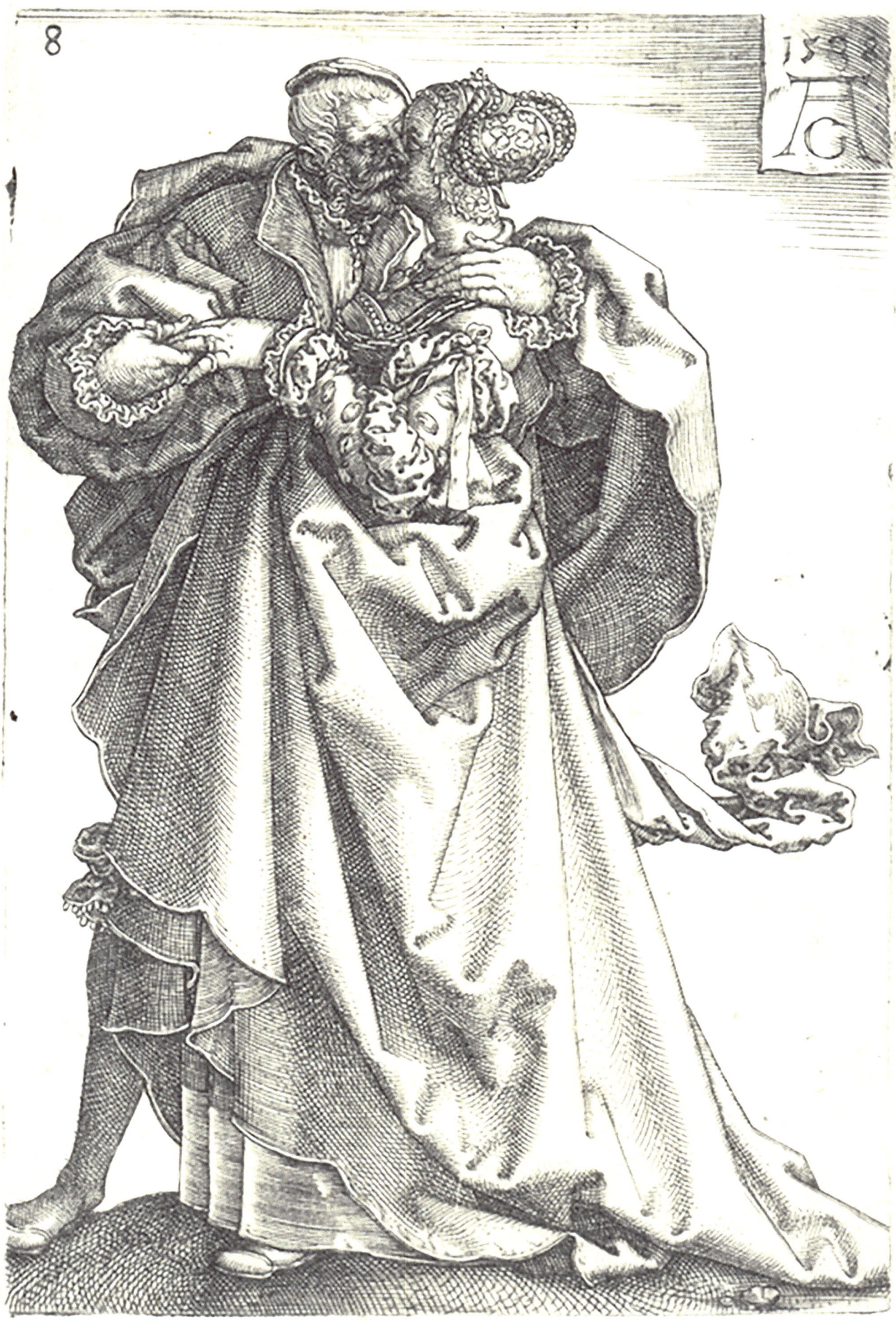

9

1538

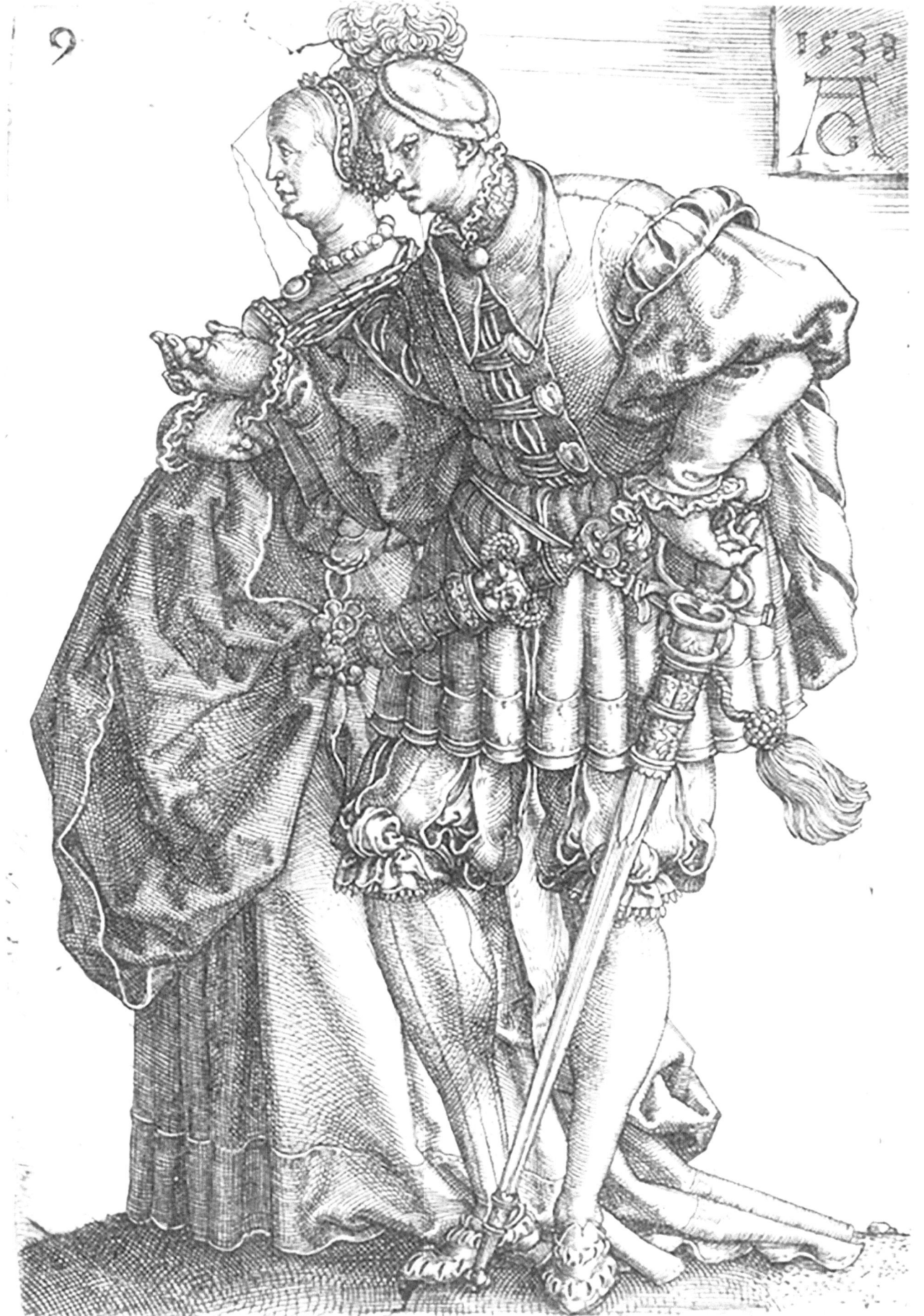

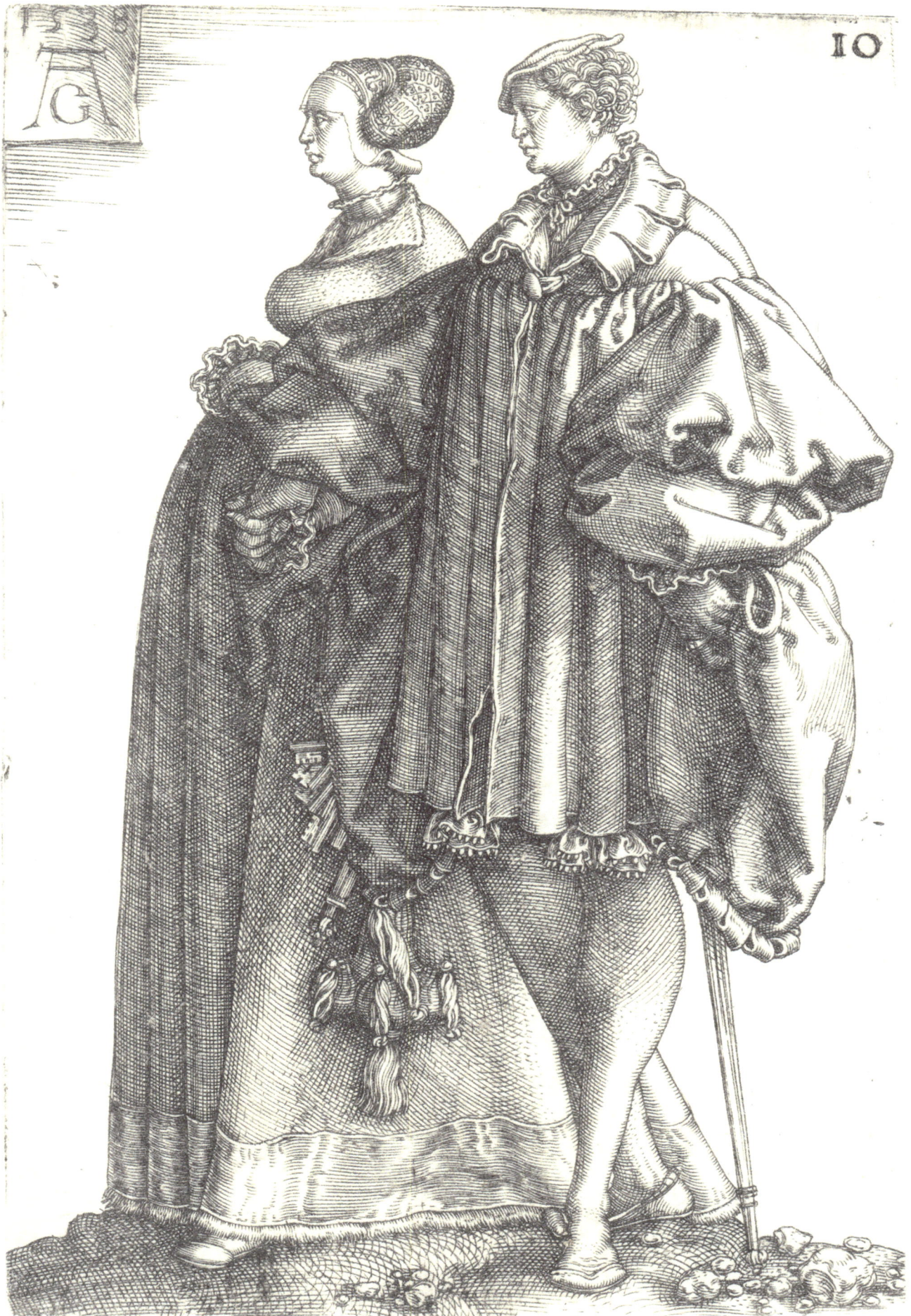

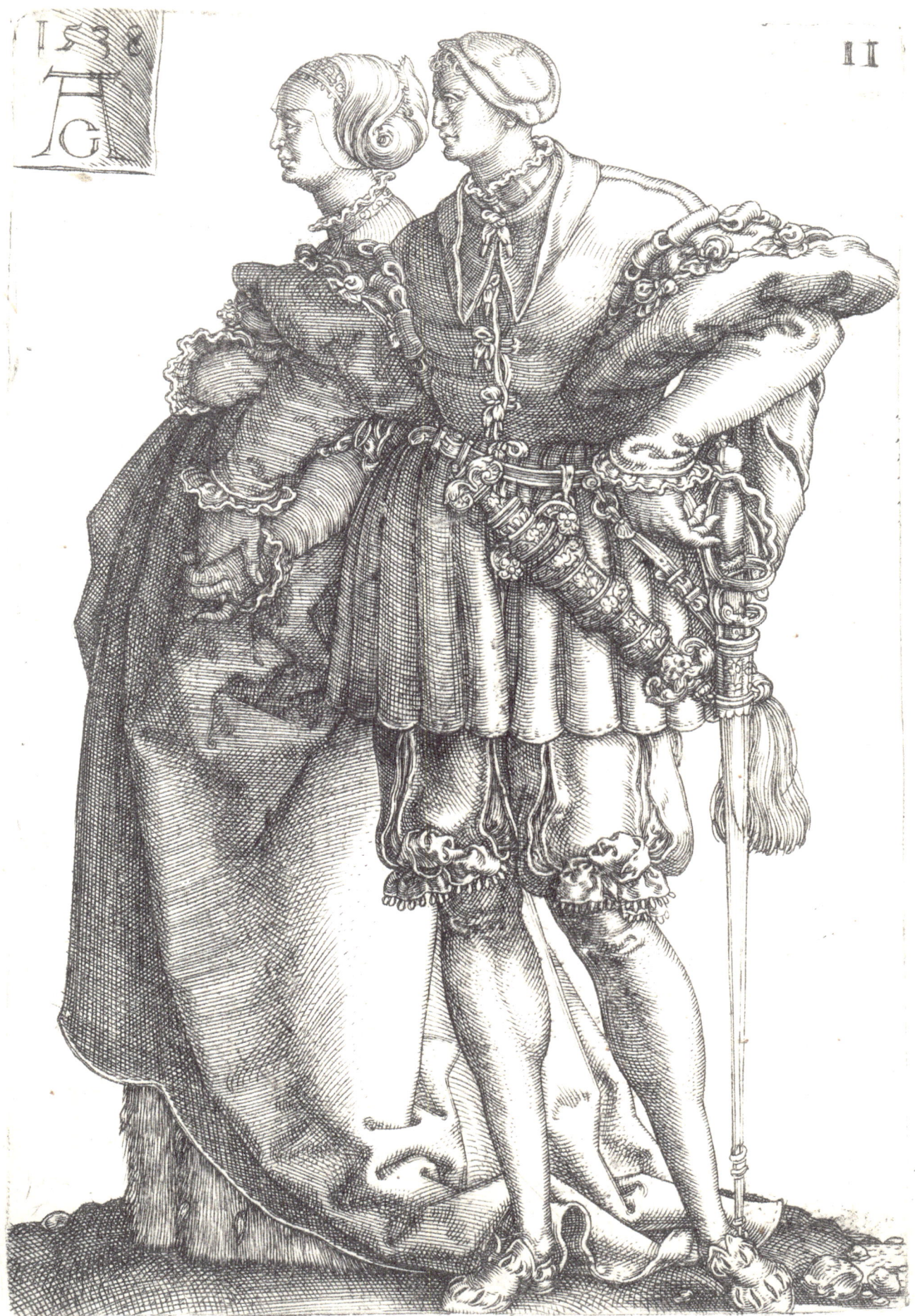

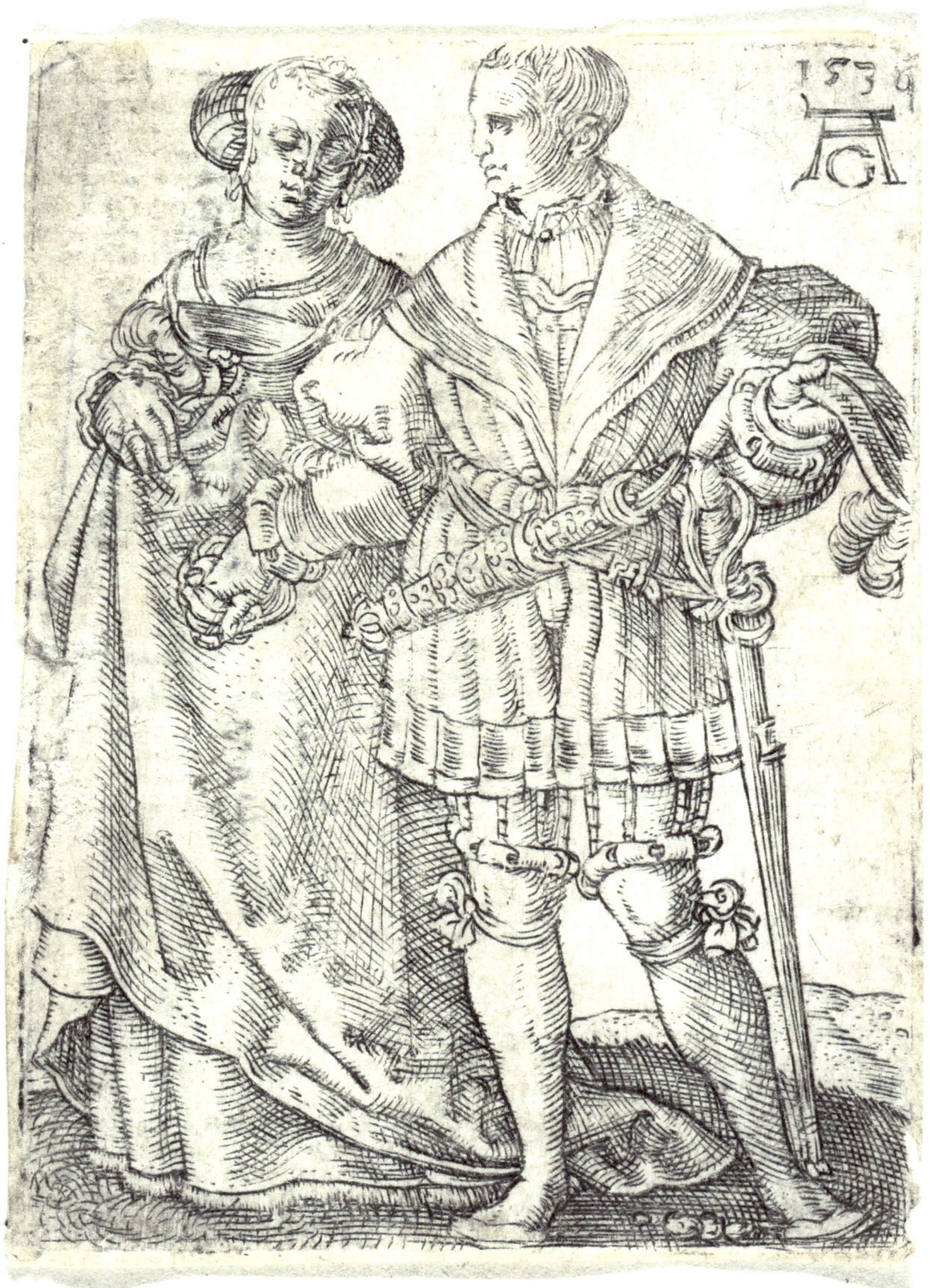

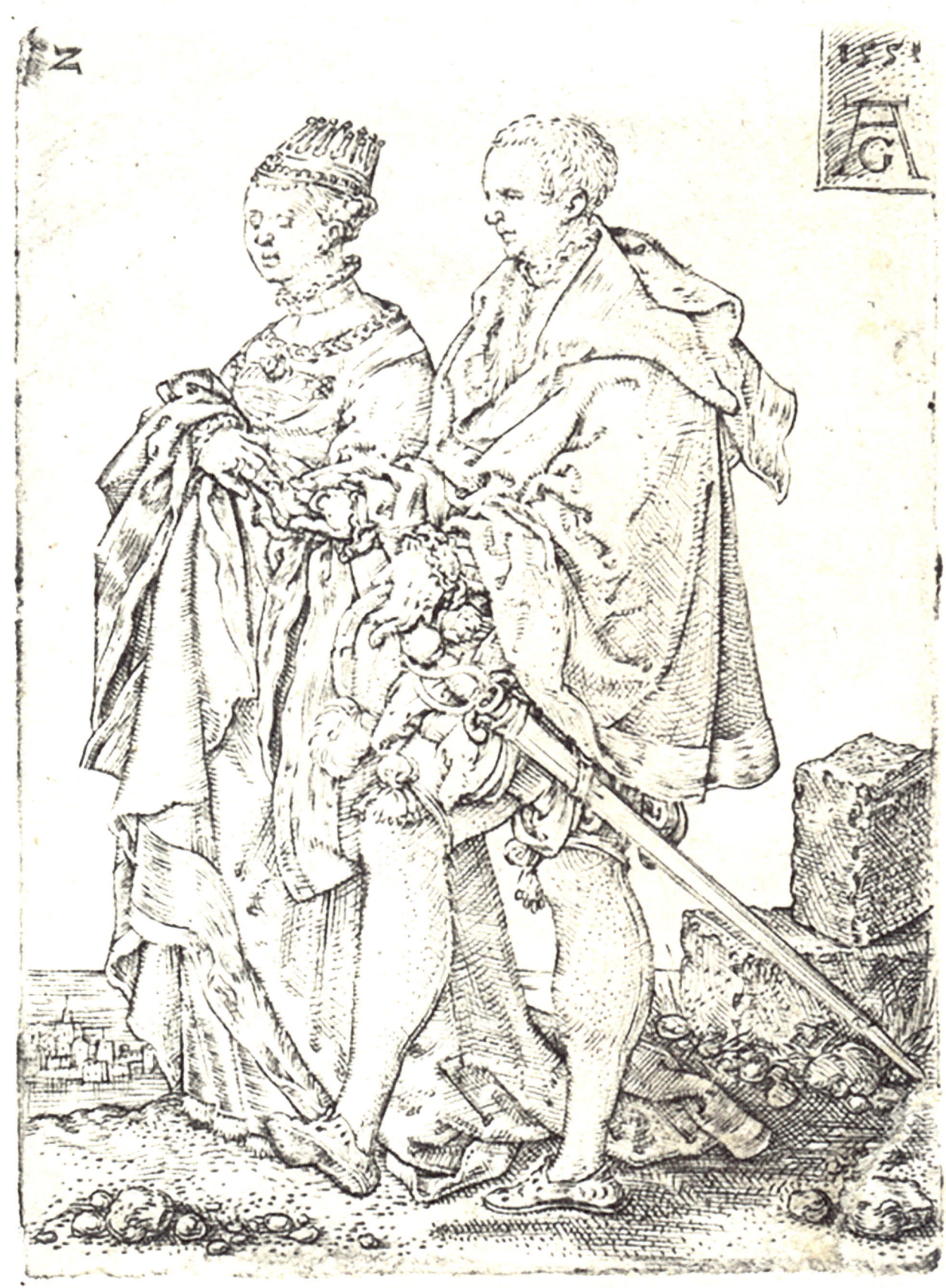

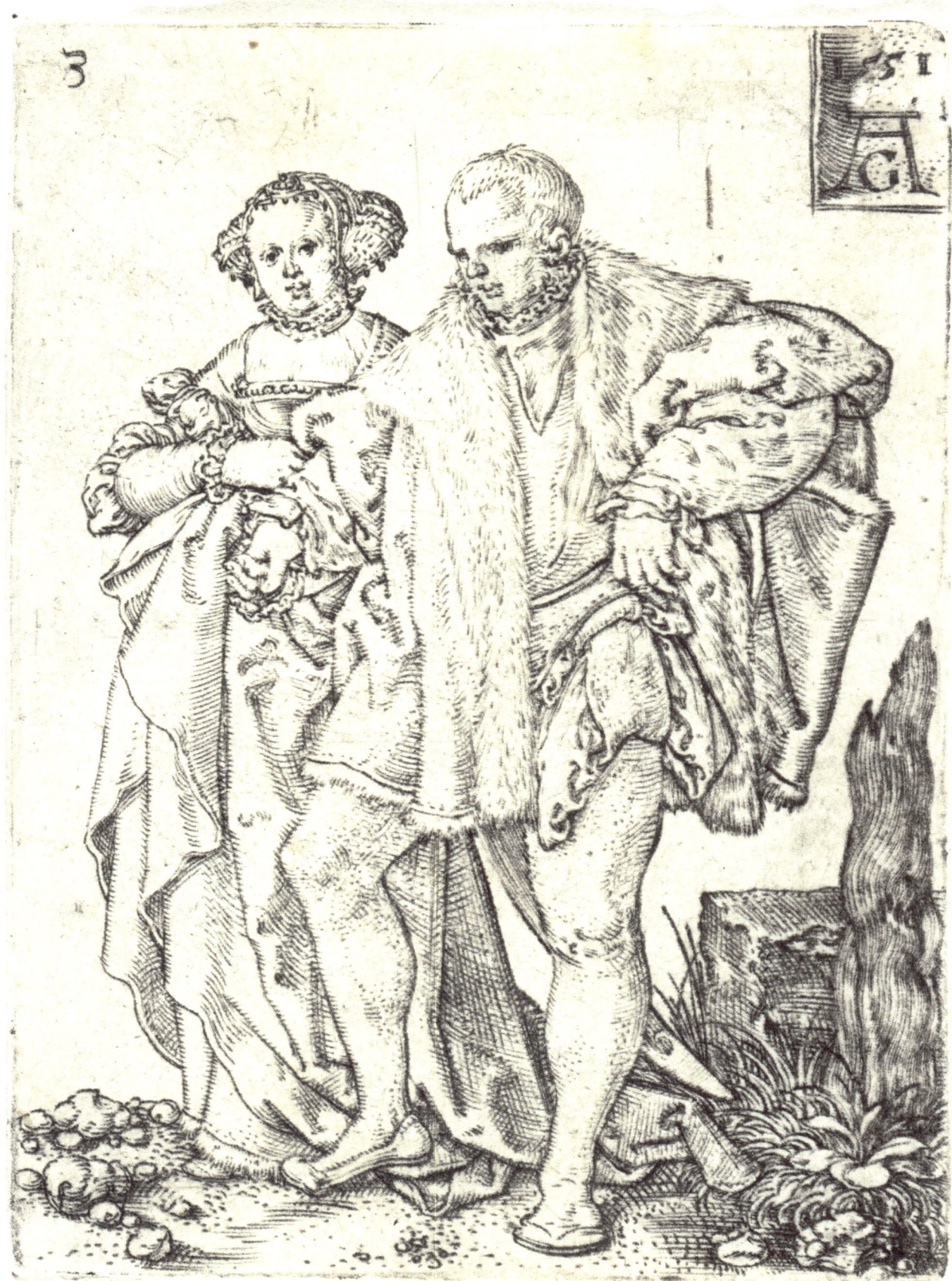

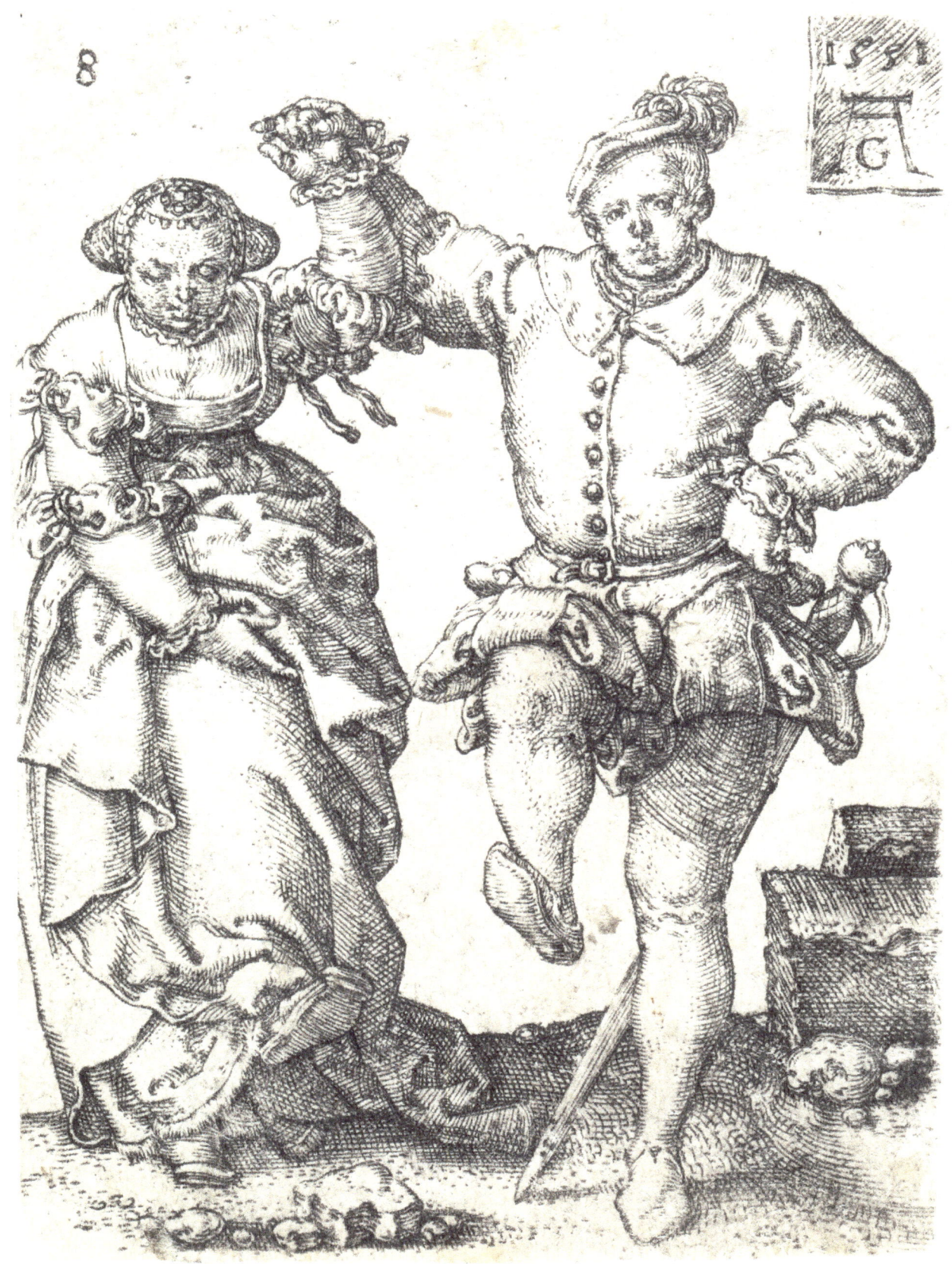

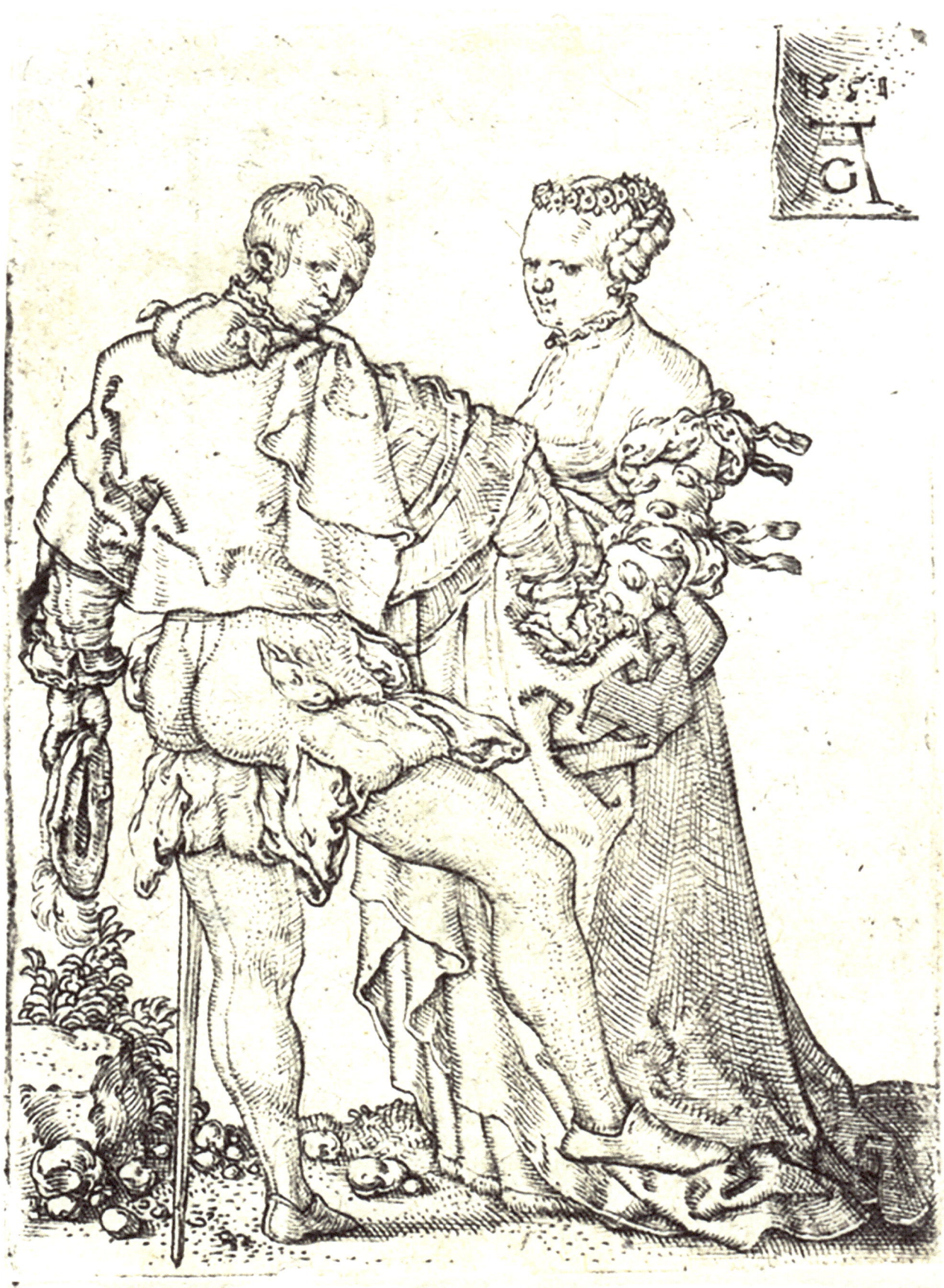

www.ingramcontent.com/pod-product-compliance
Lightning Source LLC
Chambersburg PA
CBHW050409180526
45159CB00005B/2204